Parasaurolophus
The Crested Reptile

I0440114

Dinosaur Books For Young Readers
By
Enrique Fiesta

Mendon Cottage Books

JD-Biz Publishing

Read More Amazing Animal Books

Purchase at Amazon.com

Table of Contents

Introduction 4
Chapter 1: Appearance and Behavior 7
Chapter 2: Environment 10
Conclusion 15
Author Bio 16
Bonus Dinosaur Content 17
Introduction to Dinosaurs 18
Facts about Dinosaurs 20
Dinosaur Extinction 23
Dinosaur Fossils 25
Dinosaur Eggs 26
Dinosaur Names 27
Dinosaur Diet 32
Feathered Dinosaurs 34
Plant Eating Dinosaurs 35
The Weirdest Dinosaurs 37
The Deadliest Dinosaurs 39
Flying Dinosaurs 41
Kinds of Dinosaurs 44
The Biggest Dinosaurs 47
The Smallest Dinosaurs 49
Author Bio 50
Publisher 51

Introduction

Salutations young reader! Today we are going to embark on a journey back to the age of the dinosaurs. The dinosaurs are some of the most incredible animals that ever lived on our planet. They lived nearly 200 million years ago and thrived for about 165 million years. We humans have only been around for about 60,000 years and we have only been using computers for about 75 years. The dinosaurs mysteriously became extinct and disappeared from our earth, but left their fossilized remains behind. Dinosaur fossils have been constantly discovered in human history; the Chinese thought they were dragon bones and Europeans thought they were the bones of biblical monsters. Luckily, the scientific study of dinosaurs began in between 1815-1824 with the discovery of an *Iguanodon* fossil. Since then dinosaurs have been discovered all over the world. Their immense size, strange shapes, and wonderful natures make them *inherently* worthy of interest. The study of dinosaurs requires depth of imagination, analytical skills, and thought. The many unanswered questions about their lives, behavior, and disappearance provoke the curious to seek answers and ask even more questions. I hope this book fuels your imagination and makes you want to learn even more about dinosaurs. I hope you learn to appreciate the value of the dinosaurs and that you bring a spirit of openness and wonder on your journey.

Today we will be learning about the *Parasaurolophus*. This dinosaur is a cool dinosaur to study because it was highly adaptable. This species of dinosaur survived for The Parasaurolophus also had an amazing crest on the top of its head. The purpose of this crest is currently being investigated by scientists- we are going to discuss this crest and much more including the appearance, behavior, and environment of this dinosaur. We know what we know about the dinosaurs from a variety of sources including fossils, biology, and other scientific disciplines. Fossils are the ancient remains of the dinosaurs, the most familiar being their bones. Biological science is the study of life in general, but many scientists compare the dinosaurs to modern day animals to support their theories.

Before a talk about dinosaurs can take place it is important that we discuss the theory of evolution. Evolutionary theory supposes that all the animals we know and see today are the direct descendants of animals that existed millions of years ago. The dinosaurs and other creatures that existed millions of years ago either died out or gradually changed into different animals. For instance, birds are considered to be surviving dinosaurs because their dinosaur ancestors survived the dinosaur extinction event (we will discuss this later). There are no evolutionary descendants of the *Parasaurolophus*.

Remember that any time you see an * next to the name of a dinosaur, it means that a book has been written about this dinosaur in the Dinosaur Books for Young Readers series. Any word written in bold is an important scientific term which is defined in-text. Italics are used to denote the first time a dinosaur's name is mentioned in the book.

Chapter 1: Appearance and Behavior

The Parasaurolophus is one of the most famous hadrosaurs because of its distinctive crest which the dinosaur is named after: Parasaurolophus is a combination of Greek words which literally means "beside the lizard crest." The Parasaurolophus belongs to that group of dinosaurs called the **hadrosaurs**. The hadrosaurs were **herbivorous** (plant-eating) dinosaurs with flattened jaws. These flattened jaws look much like the beaks of ducks which is why the hadrosaurs are also popularly known as the duck-billed dinosaurs. The Parasaurolophus was bulky and stout. It could grow to a length of up to 33 ft. and weigh up to 5 tons. It supported its massive weight strong legs and likely balanced itself with its tail.

The Parasaurolophus, as we have mentioned, had a distinctive crest on its head. The crest extends from the top of the head and curves over the shoulders and upper back. There are many old **hypotheses** (an educated guess backed up with scientific findings) about what the purpose of this crest was, but most have been refuted. For instance, some scientists believed that the crest was used as a snorkel when the dinosaur was underwater, but it has been discovered that there is no hole at the top of the crest and that the dinosaur was primarily **terrestrial** (lived on land). Another hypothesis is that it was used for fighting; unfortunately, this is incorrect because the crest and skull of the Parasaurolophus are far too weak for fighting. One hypothesis is that the dinosaur used its crest to communicate or make certain noises. Scientists have discovered that the crest makes a strong buzzing sound when air is blown through it.

Some scientists believe the crest was gender specific. This means that they think that only the males had crests, whereas the females lacked a crest.

Like all hadrosaurs, the Parasaurolophus had a sophisticated skull and jaws. It was able to grind and chew its food much like modern herbivorous mammals. The large long-necked **sauropods** generally swallowed their food whole. The reason the Parasaurolophus was able to chew its food is that its mouth contained **dental batteries**. The dental batteries were sets, or rows, of hundreds teeth which were constantly being replaced (a similar feature is found in sharks, because they have rows of teeth that constantly fall out only to be replaced by new teeth). The Parasaurolophus not only had dental batteries but it had a beak-like mouth which allowed it to crop, cut, and strip its food. The Parasaurolophus chewing ability meant it could eat a lot of different vegetation, since the non-chewing dinosaurs were unable to eat it. The

Parasaurolophus was able to eat food on the ground and in trees because it was able to stand up on two legs if necessary.

The Parasaurolophus likely took care of its young. Hadrosaur nesting grounds have been discovered as well as nests filled with baby hadrosaurs and food particles. This evidence suggests that hadrosaurs brought food to their young. Large groups of hadrosaurs have been found in groups, which means that they died suddenly (a volcanic eruption or a landslide could kill many dinosaurs at a time instantly). The large groups tell us that the hadrosaurs stayed together in herds. It is possible that the Parasaurolophus was also a herding dinosaur. Herding offers the herding animal protection from predators. In some cases, a predator will hesitate to attack a dinosaur when it is in a herd because the sheer numbers of the herd will frighten it.

Chapter 2: Environment

The Hadrosaurs, like all dinosaurs, lived during the **Mesozoic Era**. The Mesozoic Era began about 250 million years ago and ended about 60 million years ago. The Mesozoic Era is divided into three periods: the **Triassic**, **Jurassic**, and **Cretaceous**. Most of the dinosaurs we are familiar with lived during the Jurassic and the Cretaceous, though the ancestors of these more popular dinosaurs have their origins in the Triassic Period. The era of the dinosaurs ended at the end of the Cretaceous Period during what is called the **K-Pg extinction event**. After this event almost every single dinosaur species became extinct. The extinction of the dinosaurs was probably caused by a combination of events including disease, meteoric impacts, and climate changes.

The Parasaurolophus lived during the Late Cretaceous between the period of 83-65 million years ago. This means that the Parasaurolophus species of dinosaur survived for nearly 18 million years. Human beings have only been around for about 60,000 years, which means the Parasaurolophus thrived on earth 300 times longer than us. All

Parasaurolophus fossils have been found in North America. Late Cretaceous North America was much warmer than it is today; Antarctica didn't even exist in the Cretaceous Period! The Parasaurolophus lived in humid areas such as swamps, peat swamps, floodplains, and areas with lots of rivers. The area was covered in diverse vegetation, plants, and trees.

The Parasaurolophus did not live all by itself; in fact, it shared its environment with many other dinosaurs. Some were friendly plant eating dinosaurs, but many were **carnivores**. Carnivores are animals that hunt, kill, and eat other animals to survive. The Parasaurolophus would have had to either confront or flee from predators. Some of the dinosaurs that the Parasaurolophus lived with include the fearsome *Tyrannosaurus Rex**, the *Raptor**, and the *Triceratops.**

The Tyrannosaurus Rex was the **apex predator** of Late Cretaceous North America. An apex predator is a predator at the top of its food chain (this means that no other dinosaur hunted the T-Rex). The Tyrannosaurus could grow up to 40 ft. long and weigh as much as 7 tons. The teeth of the Tyrannosaurus were extremely large- they could grow up to 12 inches long! The Tyrannosaurs was able to crush and break bone with its powerful jaws. Tyrannosaurs hunted Parasaurolophus. If the Parasaurolophus was not close to its herd it would have been in danger, because the Tyrannosaurus could easily overcome almost any lone dinosaur. Because of the Parasaurolophus' limited ability to defend itself, it would have been easy prey for an adult Tyrannosaurus Rex.

Parasaurolophus

Raptors were also predators of the Parasaurolophus. Unlike the Tyrannosaurus, Raptors were much smaller but they were no less formidable. The Raptor that lived in North America during the Late Cretaceous was the Dromaeosaurus. The Dromaeosaurus was about 7 ft. in length and 33 lbs. in weight. Dromaeosaurus was equipped with deadly weapons including sharp hand claws, serrated teeth, and a large, sickle shaped claw on its foot. It used its sickle-claw, like a knife, to cut and slash its prey. A lone Dromaeosaurus was not large enough to take on a full-grown Parasaurolophus, but it could have hunted young Parasaurolophus or hunted in packs. It is believed by many scientists that Raptors hunted in packs. A pack of Dromaeosaurus could have surrounded a Parasaurolophus and slowly slash and bite it to death.

The Triceratops was a **quadrupedal** (four-footed) dinosaur with three sharp horns protruding from a fan shaped crest which extended from the top and sides of its head. This dinosaur had much more protection from predators than the Parasaurolophus because of its long, sharp horns. It is possible that Triceratops herded together and formed circles to defend themselves. If the tails of the Triceratops were pointed toward the center of the circle, and the faces outward, it would have formed a circle lined with sharp horns. This defense would have possibly scared away large predators like the Tyrannosaurus. It is possible that Parasaurolophus and Triceratops herded close together like modern African mammals do. This kind of behavior would have been beneficial for the Parasaurolophus since the Triceratops would have scared away many predators.

Conclusion

We have taken a trip back in time to the age of the dinosaurs. We have learned about the amazing Parasaurolophus, including what it looked like, its age and environment, and the dinosaurs it lived with. We even talked about its distinctive crest. If we use our imaginations and knowledge we can think about the dinosaurs and appreciate their mysterious existence and disappearance. When we appreciate the dinosaurs we come to appreciate the value of our own present age and all the wonderful creatures we know and love today. We should do all we can to protect our natural resources and the animals that live today because they might disappear forever just like the dinosaurs! Through the study of dinosaurs we discover how diverse and wonderful nature really is. The animals we know today, we encounter with a newfound sense of wonder- and *wonder* is of the utmost importance in any study. So make sure that you never lose your sense of wonder.

Author Bio

Enrique Fiesta

I was born in Southwest Florida and I hold a degree in Latin and Greek language and literature. In addition to my principal studies, I have also studied philosophy, history, the natural sciences, and literature. I devote the majority of my spare time to reading, writing, praying, and walking. I am currently pursuing legal studies in order to become an attorney. After I earn my law degree I intend to pursue a doctorate in philosophy, literature, and politics.

Our books are available at
1. Amazon.com
2. Barnes and Noble
3. Itunes
4. Kobo
5. Smashwords
6. Google Play Books

Bonus Dinosaur Content

Introduction to Dinosaurs   18

Facts about Dinosaurs   20

Dinosaur Extinction   23

Dinosaur Fossils   25

Dinosaur Eggs   26

Dinosaur Names   27

Dinosaur Diet   32

Feathered Dinosaurs   34

Plant Eating Dinosaurs   35

The Weirdest Dinosaurs   37

The Deadliest Dinosaurs   39

Flying Dinosaurs   41

Kinds of Dinosaurs   44

The Biggest Dinosaurs   47

The Smallest Dinosaurs   49

Introduction to Dinosaurs

We will start our journey with dinosaurs with the Tyrannosaurus Rex. The fossilized remains of the Tyrannosaurus are found in the world's biggest dig sites, which are located in Montana. Palaeontologists discover new things about dinosaurs in dig sites. Dinosaurs can be huge, weird, tiny and even wonderful. The Tyrannosaurus Rex, as we will find out, was one of the huge dinosaurs palaeontologists have discovered.

Tyrannosaurus Rex

The word dinosaur is derived from the ancient Greek words "deinos" and "saurus." These words translated into English mean "terrible lizard." Dinosaurs were creatures who dwelled on Earth and dominated the life of this planet during the Mesozoic Era which was about 65 million years ago. There were also flying and marine dinosaurs and they existed with the land-dwelling dinosaurs for about 150 million years. Dinosaurs occupied every kind of environment and climate which existed on Earth at those times. They could be about as small as the size of chicken to being 100 feet long and weighing 100 tons. Dinosaurs were one of two types: one was called Ornithischia which means bird hipped, and the other Saurischia which means lizard hipped. Dinosaurs could either be herbivorous, carnivorous or omnivorous. These are long extinct animals- there are no more dinosaurs today.

Microraptor© *Michael Rosskothen - Fotolia.com*

Facts about Dinosaurs

Have you ever heard of Dinosaurs? What are they? Here are some important facts about them.

1. Dinosaurs are reptiles that lived on earth over 230 million years ago.

2. The word Dinosaur originated from Greek words "terrible lizard."

3. Dinosaurs are extinct and cannot be found on earth alive right now, but their fossils can be extracted for study.

4. The heaviest dinosaurs weighed about 80 tons, and they are called brachiosaurs. Brachiosaurs had a height of 16 meters and a length of 26 meters.

5. Dinosaurs laid eggs which can be found in many shapes and sizes. The smallest egg of a dinosaur ever found on earth is about 3 centimeters in length and a large one was about 30cm in length.

6. When dinosaur eggs become fossils they harden like rocks but maintain their structure.

7. Troodon was probably the most intelligent dinosaur. Its cranial capacity was equal to that of an average present day mammal. It had grasping hands and stereoscopic vision.

8. Ornithomiminds were the fastest dinosaurs. They were able to reach maximum speeds of 60 kilometers per hour.

Fight between Euoplocephalus tutus and Troodon formosus

9. The oldest dinosaur bones are found in Madagascar and they are around 230 million years old.

10. Micropachycephalosaurus is the longest name of a dinosaur and it means tiny thick headed lizard .It was discovered in China.

11. Thecodontosaurus Antiquus was the oldest dinosaur to be discovered in Britain .It was discovered in 1970 in a place near Bristol. It was 2.1 meters in length.

12. Up to the present over 700 species of dinosaurs have been discovered and named. Palaeontologists are carrying out more research with the aim of discovering more.

13.108 species of dinosaurs have been discovered in Britain alone.

14. Megalosaurus was the first dinosaur to be formerly named. It was named in 1824.

Dinosaur Extinction

The term extinction is used in biology to refer to the end of a species. Dinosaurs became extinct 65 million years ago at the end of the Cretaceous period. Since this took place many years ago, it is hard for scientists to find the reason that caused the dinosaurs to become extinct. Rocks and fossils are used by scientists to find out what caused the dinosaur extinction. However, there are some plausible explanations for what could have happened.

The explanations put forward include:

Volcanic eruptions
Volcanic eruption are one of the suggested reasons. According to this suggestion, there was a lot of volcanic activity that caused changes in the weather. The dinosaurs were not able to adapt to the weather changes and so they died.

Diseases
Diseases could also have caused the death of the dinosaurs. A disease could have spread rapidly and killed them.

The Ice age
The climate of the planet occasionally becomes colder. These cold-periods are called ice ages and they might have killed off the dinosaurs if they could not survive in the colder weather.

Asteroid impact

Scientists believe that a very big asteroid hit the earth during the age of the dinosaurs. An asteroid impact could have altered weather patterns and possibly lowered the temperature of the planet. This is because an asteroid impact would have ejected tons of dust particles into the sky which would have blocked sunlight. If the sun is blocked plants cannot survive, then herbivores cannot survive, and then carnivores cannot survive.

Combined reasons or Gradual extinction

It is possible that no one factor alone was responsible for the death of the dinosaurs, but possibly a combination of volcanic eruptions, asteroid collisions, and outbreak of disease.

Dinosaur Fossils

Dinosaurs are animals that existed thousands of years ago. They are of different sizes and colors. Some have wings and other appear in their own physical appearance. Dinosaur fossils have been found all over the world.

Dinosaur Fossil

Fossils are what is left of these great animals. The bones that they left behind have been turned into rock over time. Today scientists can study these great animals by finding the fossils they left behind.

Dinosaur Eggs

Dinosaur eggs have been found all over the world. Some of them are very similar to large ostrich eggs found today. They have been fossilized over time and that is why we can still find them today. They generally tend to have more symmetry and a rounder shape than modern bird eggs. Baby dinosaurs found in fossilized eggs can be studied to learn more about the nature of these wonderful animals.

Dinosaur Egg

Dinosaur Names

The following are common dinosaur names and their meanings. Most names are coined from Greek vocabulary, but some dinosaurs are named after their place where they were discovered.

1. Albertosaurus -"Lizard of Alberta" refers to the fact that it was discovered in
Alberta.

2. Allosaurus -"Strange Lizard" due to its unusual bone structures.

3. Apatosaurus-"Deceptive Lizard" because it had bones similar to another dinosaur's bones. The confusion caused by this fact made the discoverer call the dinosaur deceptive.

4. Baryonyx -"Heavy Claw" because the first fossil to be found was a claw, and because this dinosaur's hands have large claws.

5. Brontosaurus- "Thunder Beast"

6. Coelophysis -"Hollow form"

7. Cynognathus -"Dog jawed" , because it has a jaw like a dog.

8. Deinonychus -"Terrible claw", refers to the large claws on its feet.

9. Dilophosaurus -"Two-crested lizard" because of the protuberances on its head.

10. Dimetrodon -"Two size of teeth" because it has a set of large teeth and a set of small teeth.

11. Dimorphodon- "Two types of teeth" possessed two different types of teeth, which is noteworthy for a reptile.

12. Diplocaulus- "Double stalk."

13. Diplodocus -"Double beamed lizard."

14. Dolichorhynchops -"Long-nosed snout."

15. Dromaesaurus -"Running lizard."

16. Elasmosaurus -"Thin plated lizard."

17. Gallimimus -"Bird mimic" because this dinosaur looks like a bird.

18. Giganotosaurus-"Giant lizard of south" refers to the gigantic size of this dinosaur.

19. Hesperonis- "Regal western bird."

20. Ichthyosaurus -"Fish lizard" because this dinosaur lived in the ocean.

21. Iguanodon -"Iguana tooth" the tooth of this dinosaur resembled that of an iguana.

22. Kronosaurus- "Titan lizard" refers to this dinosaur's large size.

23. Liopleurodon -"Smooth-sided teeth."

24. Maiasaurus -"Good mother lizard."

25. Megalodon -"Big-toothed shark" because this shark has enormous teeth.

26. Mosasaurus- "Meuse lizard."

27. Nothosaurus - "False lizard."

28. Ornitholestes-"Bird robber."

29. Ornithomimus-"Bird mimic" because of its bird-like appearance.

30. Oviraptor- "Egg thief" because they were believed to be taking eggs of other animals.

31. Plesiosaurs -"Close to lizard."

32. Pliosaurs -"More lizards."

33. Protoceratops-"First horn face" because of its single horn.

34. Pteradactyl- "Winged-fingered lizard" because of its long fingers which seemed to form a wing.

35. Pteranodon -"Winged, without teeth" because this dinosaur has a toothless beak and wings.

36. Quetzacoatlus- was named after the Aztec god Quetzalcoatl.

37. Saltopus -"Jumping Foot", because the first fossil found of this dinosaur was a leaping foot.

38. Spinosaurus- "Thorn lizard" because of the paddle-like spines protruding from its back.

39. Stegosaurus- "Roofed lizard" because it had bones on the back.

40. Suchomimus -"Crocodile mimic" because it looks like a crocodile in appearance.

41. Triceratops -"Three-horned face" refers to the three horns protruding from this dinosaurs head.

42. Trilobites- "Three lobes" refers to the tripartite structure of this creature's body.

43. Troodon- "Wounding tooth" refers to the dinosaur's sharp teeth.

44. Tyrannosaurus Rex -"Tyrant lizard" because this dinosaur is terrible to behold.

45. Utahraptor- "Robber from Utah", this dinosaur was named after the
place it was first discovered.

46. Velociraptor- "Speedy robber."

47. Yangchuanosaurus -"Yanchuan Lizard" because it was discovered in Yangchua.

Dinosaur Diet

The diet of an average dinosaur consisted either of plants, meat, insects, or some combination of the above. The dinosaurs which ate plants exclusively are called herbivores which literally means "plant eater." These dinosaurs ate fruit, leaves, grass, and roots from the earth and from trees. These dinosaurs possessed blunt, interlocking teeth which allowed them to easily grind up their vegetable diet. Some of these dinosaurs would eat rocks to help them digest their meals. It is speculated that these dinosaurs ate a lot, drank a lot, and slept a lot.

Other dinosaurs were carnivores which literally means "meat eater." These dinosaurs are more famous than herbivores because they are commonly depicted as the antagonists in dinosaur movies: think Tyrannosaurus Rex. Carnivores would hunt other dinosaurs down and eat them in order to feet. If they were anything like modern day predators, their primary source of food was herbivorous dinosaurs. Carnivores were built for speed and possessed sharp teeth and sharp talons. They would use their speed to catch their prey, their claws to grip the grey, and their teeth to kill their prey. Some of these predators lived in packs and they would hunt together in order to bring down large prey they would otherwise not be able to kill.

Omnivores were dinosaurs which ate meat, insects, and vegetation. Omnivore literally means "all-eater." These dinosaurs would generally eat whatever was commonly available and sometimes they were scavengers. Scavengers eat the remains of animals which were killed by carnivores. These dinosaurs were specially adapted because they could survive in environments where other dinosaurs would die. If an area lacked meat or vegetation, an omnivore would survive but a herbivore or carnivore would die because of lack of food.

Feathered Dinosaurs

Shandong Tianyu Museum's discovery of partial pieces of fossils suggest that certain dinosaurs had feathers. A small skeleton of a dinosaur discovered later proved that the museum was correct. The fossil possessed feathers. Now scientists are speculating that a large variety of dinosaurs possessed feathers and these discoveries back up scientist's claims that some dinosaurs evolved into modern-day birds. Many of these feathered fossils are being discovered in China. These feathered dinosaurs possessed very complex and unique teeth. They were pointed, sharp, and peculiarly large. The teeth in their back jaws were broad and flat. Their teeth seem to indicate that they were able to eat both meat and vegetation, thus making them omnivores.

Plant Eating Dinosaurs

Herbivorous dinosaurs were well adapted to eating plants because of their teeth and long neck. Their teeth were built specially for grinding down plant matter, and some dinosaurs had long necks which allowed them to eat from the tops of trees. The following dinosaurs are common herbivorous dinosaurs.

1. Sauropodomorphs

They are also known as prosauropods. They consist of dinosaurs such as Plateosaurus ,Massopondylus, Lufengosaurus and Anchisaurus. They were
able to feed on trees up to a height of 1.2 meters. They had well adapted teeth which were roughened and diamond shaped which allowed for easy tearing of vegetation. They had thick muscles at the gizzards that helped to break down the food.

2. Ornithischains

They had horny peak that was sharp and protruding out of the mouth for cropping plants. Teeth were adapted for tearing the picked plant food before swallowing. They had a fleshy cheek which covered parts of the side of their mouths. In this group there were dinosaurs such as lesothosaurus, Orodromes and the
Scelosaurus.

3. Larger ornithopods

They included dinosaurs such as Ouranosaurus, Iguanodonand, Hadrosaurus. They had a beak which was sharp and broad for picking plant foods. They had interlocking teeth which allowed them to tear vegetation easily.

4. Larger ceratopians

They had extremely narrow beak which resembles that of a parrot. The beak was used to feed on vegetation by cutting the vegetation. They had more than one hundred teeth behind the beak; the teeth were interlocking for easy chewing of the plants picked. Psittacosaurus was a ceratopian.

The Weirdest Dinosaurs

Let's discuss a few of the weirdest dinosaurs known to humans.

Oviraptor- This dinosaur looked very similar to a modern day ostrich.
Oviraptor was weird in the sense that it already had bird like features before it became extinct.

Ouranosaurs- They had spines coming out of their backbone which means it had a sail on its back, or a large hump of flesh like a modern day camel. Since it was discovered in a desert, it is possible that it was a camel-like dinosaur.

Carnotaurus- Looked like a tiny Tyrannosaurs Rex. The Carnotaur had horns on its eyebrows and incredibly tiny arms.

Mamenchisaurus was herbivore but what made it weird was the length of its neck. It had an enormous 35-40 foot neck and not
surprisingly, it could never stretch it to full length upwards but had to carry it parallel to the ground.

The Deadliest Dinosaurs

Here are some of the deadliest dinosaurs. These dinosaurs were the lions, tigers, and bears of their time, only much, much larger.

1.Tyrannosaurus Rex
It had numerous strong and sharp teeth. This dinosaur was incredibly large and was probably the apex predator wherever it lived.

2. Utahraptor dinosaur
It had single curved claws which looked like a knife attached to its feet. These dinosaurs might have hunted in packs which made bringing down prey an easier task.

3 Jeholopterus
This dinosaur had sharp fangs. It is believed that the Jeholopterus made a living by sucking blood from other dinosaurs such as large sauropods (long-neck dinosaurs).

4. Kronosaurus
This is believed to have been bigger than the present great white shark. It possessed bigger teeth and a bigger jaw size. Think of a whale-sized shark coming after you.

5. Allosaurus
The Allosaurus was a fierce predator. This is proven by its very powerful jaws and sharp claws.

6. Sarcosuchus

This was the largest crocodile of the dinosaur age. Its length was double that of the largest crocodiles today and its weight was equal to 10 modern-day crocodiles. It had a long and powerful neck which allowed it to jump out of the water with lightning-quick speed.

7. Giganotosaurus

It had a weight of about 8 tons and three strong fingers on each of its hands. It was the largest predator that ever existed on earth. A full grown Gigantosaurus was probably able to bring down full-grown sauropods (long-neck dinosaurs).

Flying Dinosaurs

There are several species of dinosaurs which could fly or glide. Here are four of the flying dinosaurs that inhabited the earth millions of years ago.

Dimorphodon is one of the flying dinosaurs that existed during the age of reptiles. This type of dinosaur had two kinds of teeth and it was around 3.3 feet in length with a wing span of 4 feet. Due to its inability to stand and walk, this dinosaur spent a lot of time perched when not flying.

Dimorphodon

Rhamphorhynchus in another flying dinosaur that had short legs, a long tail that was made of ligaments, and a wing span of 3 feet in length. It had a narrow jaw with very sharp teeth and had a beak which it probably used to catch fish.

Rhamphorhynchus

The *Quetzalcoatlus* was discovered in North America and it is known to be one of the largest flying reptiles during the time dinosaurs were living on earth. Its wing span was 36 feet in length, and it had large eyes, a crested head, a very thin beak and its weight is speculated to have been around 300 pounds. The bones of this flying dinosaur were hollow which meant it could fly for very long distances.

Quetzalcoatlus

The *Pterodactyus* lived near water and its diet consisted of fish and other kinds of small animals. Its wing span was 20 to 30 inches.

Kinds of Dinosaurs

There were many different types of dinosaurs. Here is how scientists have classified them.

Dino Basics

A famous British scientist named Harry Seeley, in 1800's proposed a classification based on their hip structure. Seeley classified two major groups called Ornithischia (bird-hipped) and Saurischia (lizard-hipped). These two types were further broken down into sub groups as follows:

Ornithischia

Thyreophora: Also known as the armored dinosaurs, these dinosaurs were herbivores (plant eaters) and lived in the early Jurassic to the late Creaceous age. Thyrephora simply means "shield bearers" because these type of dinosaurs had armor, plates and horns. This group included Stegosaurus, Ankylosaurusand Nodosauus.

Ornithischia

Cerapods: These are typically horned or duck-billed dinosaurs Just like the Thyreophora, Cerapods were herbivores however, these dinosaurs has better teeth that helped them grind plants better. Cerapods were able to extract more nutrients from their food because of their more advanced jaws.

Saurischia
Theropods: The name means "beast feet." Typically, these dinosaurs moved on two legs and were carnivores (meat eaters). Some of these kinds of dinosaurs were also omnivores (ate both plants and meat). Theropods lived from the late Triassic period until the end of Cretaceous period. Scientists have also discovered that birds are the evolved-descendants of Theropods. While the scary looking and most popular ones in this category are the Tyrannosaurus Rex and Veliociraptor, there were also other dinosaurs like Spinosaurus, Deinonychus, Allosaurus, Carnotaurus,

Albertosaurus, Megalosaurus, Yangchuanosaurus and much more.

Sauropods: These lizard-footed type of dinosaurs walked on four legs and were enormous in size. They had long necks and tails, were huge in size and had comparatively small heads. Sauropods were herbivores and included Brachiosaurus, Diplodocus, Seismosaurus, Giraffatitan, and Apatosaurus.

The Biggest Dinosaurs

During the Jurassic period there were many heavy, gigantic dinosaurs that roamed all throughout the earth. Some of the biggest dinosaurs are listed below:

Liopleurodon - Liopleurodon looked similar to an orca and a shark, and it was the biggest pliosaur. It had a massive body, huge flippers, and a long thick jaw full of teeth. Palaeontologists say that this type of dinosaur weighed over 30 tons and could grow to a length of 50 feet.

Quetzalcoatlus - This type of dinosaur was also huge in size as it had a wingspan of 45 feet. This huge pterosaur has received its name from the winged Aztec god.

Spinosaurus - Spinosaurus was heavier than Tyrannosaurus Rex and it is believed that they were bigger in size too. It had a mouth that was similar to crocodile's mouth and it also had a skin flap that protruded from its back which resembled a sail. It is believed that the sail helped the dinosaur regulate its body temperature.

Argentinosaurus - As the name suggests, the fossils of this dinosaur was found in Argentina. It was among the biggest dinosaurs with weight of over 100 tons and height of up to 120 feet. A single spinal vertebra is four feet in diameter.

Argentinosaurus

The Smallest Dinosaurs

Fossils have helped palaeontologists discover the smallest dinosaurs that lived on earth. They are as follows: The Humming Bird - It may seem strange, but palaeontologists believe that dinosaurs did not become extinct completely but underwent evolution. Humming birds are believed to be the evolutionary descendants of dinosaurs that lived millions of years ago. It weighs as little as one-tenth of an ounce, and is considered to be the smallest dinosaur species that lives today.

Lariosaurus - With a total weight of about 20 pounds and a length of 2 feet, this dinosaur was the smallest aquatic dinosaur. It had a long pointed tail and a streamlined body. It usually lived in water but it also dwelt on land. It was similar to amphibians because it could live in both environments.

Pterosaurus - Pterosaurus had hollow bones and were lightly built. The pterosaurs were of different sizes but the smallest one was just a few inches long. This carnivorous dinosaur ate insects, crabs and fishes.

Microceratops - The microceratops was the smallest herbivorous dinosaur. It weighed 4 pounds and had a height of about a foot and a half.

Microaptor - The microaptors were the smallest carnivorous dinosaurs. They had a height of just 2 feet from head to tail. They were also known as "four-winged dinosaur" because they had feathers on their legs and arms. Their diet consisted only of insects.

Author Bio

Enrique Fiesta

I was born in Southwest Florida and I hold a degree in Latin and Greek language and literature. In addition to my principal studies, I have also studied philosophy, history, the natural sciences, and literature. In my spare time I devote the vast majority of my time to reading, writing, praying, and walking. I am currently pursuing legal studies in order to become an attorney. After I earn my law degree I intend to pursue a doctorate in philosophy, literature, and politics.

Our books are available at
1. Amazon.com
2. Barnes and Noble
3. Itunes
4. Kobo
5. Smashwords
6. Google Play Books

Publisher

JD-Biz Corp

P O Box 374

Mendon, Utah 84325

http://www.jd-biz.com/

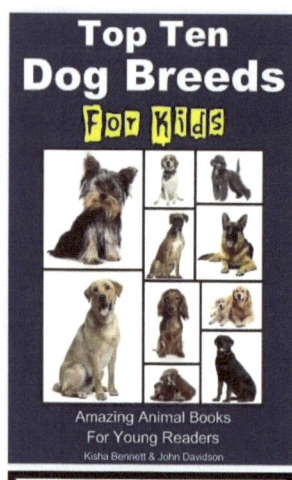

Top Ten Dog Breeds For Kids

Amazing Animal Books
For Young Readers
Kisha Bennett & John Davidson

Poodles

Dog Books for Kids
K. Bennett

Labrador Retrievers

Dog Books for Kids
K. Bennett

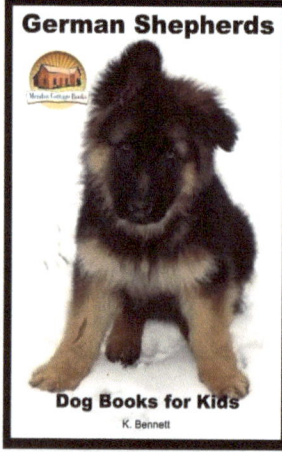

German Shepherds

Dog Books for Kids
K. Bennett

Rottweilers

Dog Books for Kids
K. Bennett

Boxers

Dog Books for Kids
K. Bennett

Golden Retrievers

Dog Books for Kids
K. Bennett

Beagles

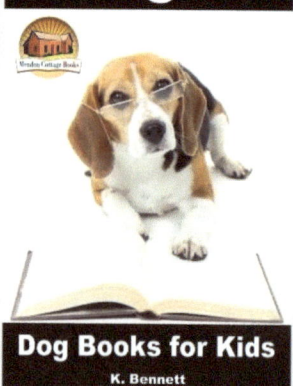

Dog Books for Kids
K. Bennett

Yorkies

Dog Books for Kids
K. Bennett

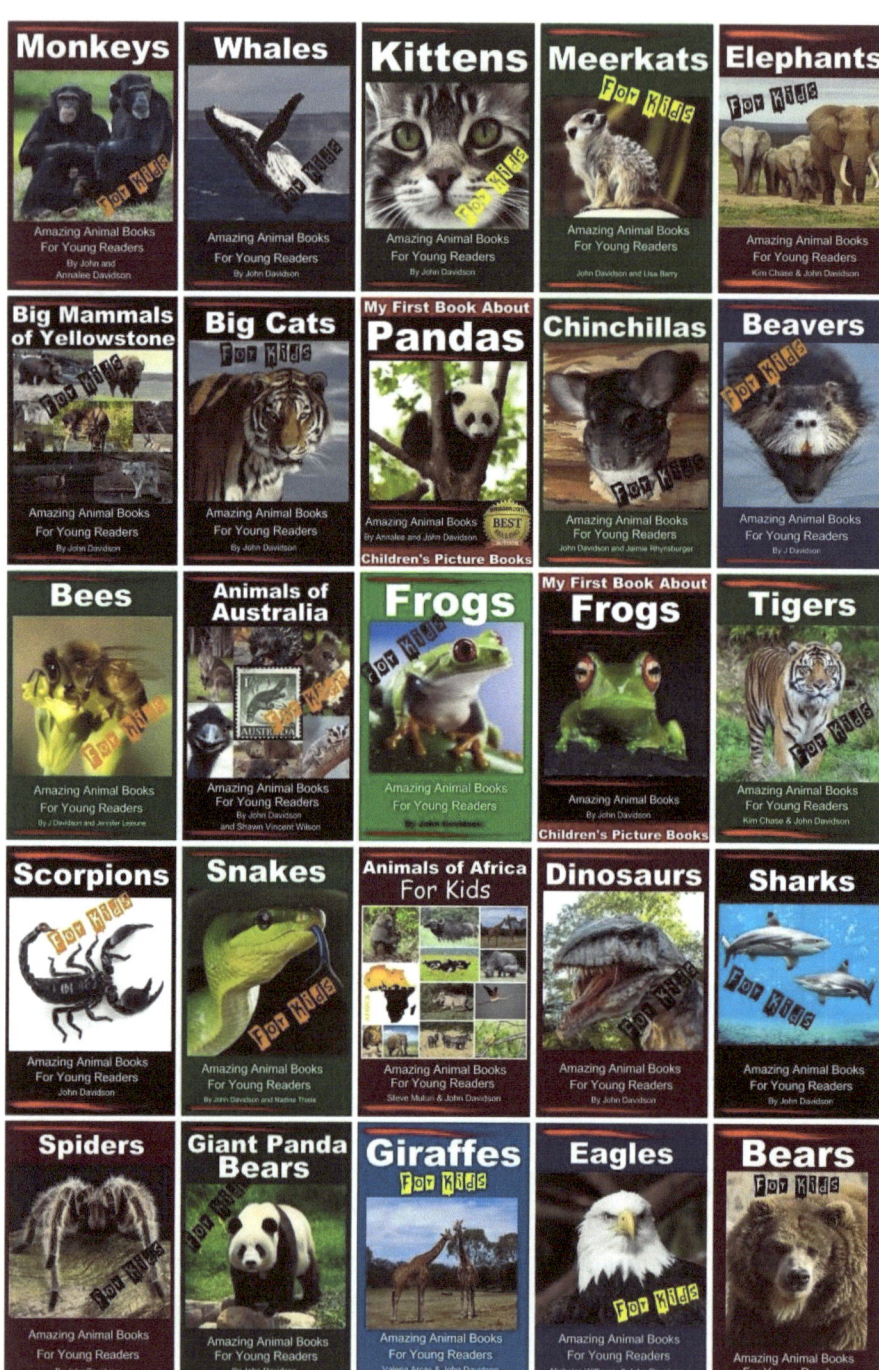

www.ingramcontent.com/pod-product-compliance
Lightning Source LLC
Chambersburg PA
CBHW040746010626
45792CB00027B/296